Lancashire Legends

Lancashire Legends

by Kathleen Eyre

illustrated by
Bruce Danz

Dalesman Books
1972

The Dalesman Publishing Company Ltd.
Clapham (via Lancaster), Yorkshire
First published 1972

© *Text Kathleen Eyre* 1972
©*Illustrations Bruce Danz* 1972

ISBN: 0 85206 153 6

Printed in Great Britain by Galava Printing Co. Ltd.,
Hallam Road, Nelson, Lancs.

Contents

The cover illustration is of Carr House, Bretherton

Introduction

THIS COLLECTION of Lancashire legends casts its net wide over the Red Rose county and comes up with tales from most of the ancient Hundreds, from Lonsdale in the north to West Derby in the south, from the shores of Amounderness in the west to the boundaries of old Salford Hundred in the south-east.

It is a selection. Only a volume of gigantic proportions could embrace all the folk-tales which thrilled our forebears and set their pulses racing. Many indeed have passed into oblivion, obliterated with the ancient walls to which they were attached. Others died with their narrators who were in the habit of repeating them orally to succeeding generations. Nevertheless, the general decline of interest in old ways and old pleasures in this technological age (which must have proof of everything before it can believe!) does not, fortunately, apply to tenacious Lancashire. This county, perhaps more than any other in England, clings persistently to its ancient stories and traditions, perpetuates the old customs and attaches itself with affection to folk-lore and ballad. From practically every hall and hamlet, township or hillock, from every bridge or river, clough or dell, from every hostelry or farmstead with a few genera-tions of history, some marvellous tale springs forth from olden times. Often far-fetched and invested with a high degree of improb-ability, yet it is still possible, at times, to discern a fine thread of truth gleaming through the fabulous.

No-one can say how these legends took their rise. Their origin is obscured by the mists of a far distant and superstitious past. Nevertheless, they reveal ancient attitudes, shed light on the beliefs and manners of a bygone age and allow us to peep into an era before the benefits of universal education, before mass communication by press, radio and television, and before mass entertainment in cinema and theatre. For our ancestors, the age-old habit of telling tales enlivened a penurious existence, provided an escape from harrowing and hum-drum routine and satisfied the deep basic human need for a story.

Fortunately, the true Lancastrian was ever a good talker, a splendid teller of tales, with a sharp wit and a flair for dramatic inflection to colour his recollections. Seated in his massive elbow chair in the chimney corner, he delighted in spinning out titillating yarns to an audience thirsting greedily after the sensational. All the ingredients were available to the Lancastrian retailer of legends— severed hands, severed heads, ghostly horsemen, wicked uncles, foul murderers, oppressive landowners and supposed witches. White ladies floated abundantly about the Tudor halls of Roman Catholic Lancashire, as might be expected in the county which, above all others, remained steadfast to the old faith throughout the prolonged period of persecution. A ghost was a convenient cover-up for illegal priestly sojourns, for secret and highly dangerous comings and goings. The invented "White Lady" accounted for unexplained noises in the night, allayed the suspicions of servants in those tension- packed and nerve-stretching times but, having been invented, she passed into tradition and remained at her post long after toleration was practised.

The dreadful appearance of some local apparition, the portentous predictions of the rustic seer, and natural phenomena which could not then be explained, figured in the constant topics of discourse within the old-time domestic circle, evoking a sharp thrill of nervous excitement and pleasure. Nor were charming tales of the "little people" overlooked in an age which feasted on charms, spells, omens and superstitions. Dwarfs, elves and fairies skip happily through many old Lancashire fables.

But of all the tribe of phantasmal little haunting creatures, perhaps the boggart was best beloved in John o' Gaunt's domain. Boggarts came in all shapes and sizes, some mini-human, others in animal guise. There were genial boggarts and spiteful boggarts, those who would help with the work, others who smashed crockery and tor- mented hapless humans. Black-dog boggarts prowled the county (there was one at Warton, near Preston), and a hairy boggart at nearby Weeton terrified the good-folk of the village. There were boggarts with cloven-hooves and boggarts in the form of cats, or pigs or spectral horses. It was all good, meaty, highly-flavoured material with the power to invoke a state of delicious apprehension.

Old Nick was pretty active, too, though he met his match on several occasions in Lancashire. It was a matter for great hilarity and self-congratulation that the Devil was bested by native wit when he failed to accomplish the impossible tasks set by clever folk at Hothersall, Clitheroe and Cockerham. Old Nick himself could not twist an enduring rope out of fine sand, and our ancestors had a good laugh at his expense.

Many more deserved to be included which may perhaps be recorded at some future time. Meantime, this random collection of long-loved tales is commended to your enjoyment in the spirit of Francis Bacon, who wrote:

"Out of monuments, names, traditions, private records and evidences, fragments of stories, and the like, we do save and recover somewhat from the deluge of time."

1

North Lancashire

Lancaster—John o' Gaunt's Horse Shoe.

IN THE CENTRE of the junction formed by Penny Street, Cheapside and St. Nicholas Street, Lancaster, a horse-shoe set in the roadway is that traditionally cast by John o' Gaunt's steed. It has, of course, been renewed from time to time. John of Gaunt built the famous Gateway Tower of Lancaster Castle which was his palace. His son, Henry IV, linked the Duchy with the Crown.

"Snatchems"—The Golden Ball.

LEAVING Skerton Bridge via the Heysham Road and Ovangle Road, the quiet way over the marshes to Overton and Sunderland Point takes the traveller past an interesting public house called The Golden Ball, but better known as "Snatchems." The high-water mark, above car-roof height, painted on the wall overlooking the car park is a daunting reminder of the need to be wary of the tides. "Snatchems" is grimly reminiscent of the press-gangs whose ruthless methods provided crews for the tall-masted ships sailing from Sunderland Point.

Sunderland Point, Sambo's Grave and the Cotton Tree.

THOUSANDS of visitors come annually to this delightful little community, on the Lune Estuary, which twice a day is cut off by the tides. Sunderland Point was once the fourth largest port in the country. Tall-masted ships from America and the West Indies brought cotton and romantic cargoes of rum, tobacco and sugar to the merchants of Lancaster. Raw cotton was imported here before it came into Liverpool. There was also a lively traffic in slaves.

Early in the 18th century, Sambo, a negro slave, arrived at Sunderland Point with his master, a ship's captain who hastened off to Lancaster to treat with his proprietors. Black Sambo died, some said, of a broken heart, thinking himself deserted. Others hinted at

Above: The "Cotton Tree" at Sunderland Point. Opposite: The Old Roof Tree Inn. St. Patrick's Chapel, Heysham.

murder though Sambo, quite as likely, expired of a fever or pneumonia. It was considered improper to bury him alongside decent Christians and, instead, Sambo was laid to rest on the lonely shore. His grave has become a place of pilgrimage. Tended and flower-bedecked by the children of the Point, it can be found over a low wall by walking up Church Lane to the far shore and proceeding left for about 200 yards. A brass plate (later defaced), let into the tombstone, bore the moving message:

> *Here lies poor Sambo,*
> *A faithful negro, who*
> *attending his master*
> *from the West Indies, died on his*
> *arrival at Sunderland.*

A second plate was affixed, bearing a poem, part of which runs:

> *Full sixty years the angry winter's wave*
> *Has, thundering dashed this bleak and barren shore*
> *Since Sambo's head laid in this lonely grave*
> *Lies still and ne'er will hear their turmoil more.*

(1796)

Another curiosity at Sunderland Point, which declined after Glasson Dock was opened in 1787, is the famous "Cotton Tree." It is a kapok tree, in fact, and an arresting sight in summertime. The old warehouses and cottages, bearing ancient dates, the charming

homes of long-forgotten sea captains and the "Bath House" (now a garage) where slaves and seamen were de-loused after their voyagings, make Sunderland Point another little world of welcome serenity in these hurried days.

Middleton Old Hall, Near Heysham.

DURING the reign of Edward III the monks of Cockersand Abbey received the gift of Middleton township and manor, near Heysham. The original manor house was replaced about 1440 by one known today as the Old Roof Tree Inn. It was formerly Middleton Old Hall, and was acquired by the Dalton family after the Dissolution. It was customary in those times to erect houses upon a framework of cruck timbers. Visible in the domestic quarters of the inn are the massive tree trunks which support the building, hence its modern name.

During restoration work, an ancient key was discovered beneath the threshold stone, a quaint reminder of the superstitious belief in the power of witches in earlier centuries. It was thought that a lump of cold metal, such as a key, was a protection against hags. The precaution might have been taken in 1612 when the Pendle witches were hauled up to Lancaster for trial and execution. The key is on view in the bar.

Heysham—St. Patrick's Chapel

A MASS OF legend surrounds the life of St. Patrick who was a Roman, born late in the 4th century, probably at Kilpatrick on Clydeside. In youth he was captured by Pictish pirates, taken to Ireland and enslaved by an Irish chieftain. His solitary duties as shepherd evoked deep contemplation and an urge to convert the Irish to the Christian faith, which he was later to accomplish. At length he escaped from captivity, took ship with a few comrades and set out for home.

The frail barque foundered on St. Patrick's Skier, a stanner near Heysham Head, and upon coming ashore St. Patrick found himself in a hotbed of Druidism. He met the challenge by fearlessly proclaiming his Christian message before pressing on with his party, on foot, to the Clyde. Between the 6th and 7th centuries, St. Patrick's Chapel was erected where traditionally the saint came ashore. It was possibly built by Celtic missionaries who came over from Ireland to secure the north-west for Christ.

It was a small, sturdy building, measuring 24 ft. by 8 ft., with walls roughly 30 ins. thick, only two of which still remain. There was no east window. About the year 900 marauding Vikings despoiled and unroofed the chapel and in 967 a new church, dedicated, to St. Peter, was built in the sheltered hollow below the chapel ruins. In 1967 St. Peter's Church, Heysham, marked 1,000 years of church history with summer-long celebrations.

Heysham—The Hog Backed Stone

ONE OF Heysham's most interesting antiquities is the fine hog-backed stone which is now protectively housed within the church. These stones are rare and the good condition of Heysham's specimen is due to its having lain buried for centuries until it was accidentally uncovered in the churchyard about 1800. Nearby was a rusty spearhead, suggesting that the curiously carved stone commemorated some ancient warring chieftain. One legend suggests that Torrig, who gave his name to Torrisholme, erected this memorial to a respected foe, the Saxon chief Eagle. Antiquarians from far afield have attempted to decipher the ornamental carvings on this fascinating relic from the distant past.

Heysham—Stone Coffins

SIX STONE COFFINS hewn in a row out of the solid rock of the headland beside St. Patrick's Chapel, Heysham, have excited much curiosity. (Two smaller specimens are to be found to the east of the hill). These last resting places of ancient Heysham notables are difficult to date, being rare in this country. They are possibly the

Top: The remains of the building. Bottom: The six stone coffins beside the chapel.

same age as the chapel. Each was hollowed out in the shape of a human body, having a groove to accommodate a stone lid and a square socket above each head, into which, presumably, a cross of wood or stone was slotted. This unusual mode of burial was obviously confined to important people. Humbler folk were interred in the "Barrows" nearby.

Heysham - The Druid's Stone.

THIS CAN STILL be seen, though hidden among foliage, about halfway up the rocky cliff behind the garden of Heysham Rectory.

Silverdale to Arnside—Fairy Steps and Pele Towers.

WANDER westwards from the old church at Beetham and take the

Fairy Steps, near Arnside.

signposted path to the Fairy Steps or, if you are more energetic, stride out from Silverdale over to Arnside and Hazelslack. This is an enchanted land, a "fairy little domain" of limestone scars, deeply scored an fissured, thinly overlaid with soil and close-cropped turf, with woodlands and clearings and an embroidery of sweet wild flowerets.

The steps are solid and ordinary enough, cut into a cleavage of the rocks, but do not doubt their fairy origin for it was believed that the fairies once skipped up and down them in their comings and goings. So did local folk on their way to Beetham Church but not with the same ease in this constricted flue. If you make a wish and can proceed up the steps without assistance and without touching the sides, it is said to come true. But this is an exercise strictly for weight-watchers.

While in the district, make a point of visiting two border pele towers which recall the lawless plunderings of Scottish raiders. Their wild surprise attacks were a sad feature of 14th century life. They drove away beasts, sheep and horses and took forth "of divers families all, the very rackencrooks and pothooks." Afterwards, the local people crept back from their towers of refuge to homes ruined and despoiled by the invaders. Arnside Tower was built by the Stanleys as a defence. Three walls of this gaunt limestone ruin stand proudly erect; the fourth keeled over in 1602, smitten by a mighty wind, followed by a fire. Hazelslack, flanked by farm buildings, is another 14th century pele tower not far from the Fairy Steps. It was the refuge of the Thwengs and their dependants from the Caledonian marauders long ago.

Warton's Stars and Stripes.

EVERY YEAR, on Independence Day, the American flag is flown at St. Oswald's Church at Warton the village near Carnforth. It is a fitting gesture, since the inspiration for the famous "Stars and Stripes" was taken from the coat of arms of the Washington family, natives of that parish from the 15th century. George Washington first President of the U.S.A., was descended from John Washington of Warton who emigrated to Virginia in the mid-17th century.

Many American tourists visit Warton to see Washington House in Main Street and the much-weathered tablet bearing the coat of arms which is now housed inside the tower of the church. Warton produced another family famous in history—the Spencers who became the great Churchills. Far back in history, the two families were linked by marriage, making George Washington and Winston Churchill distant relatives.

Aughton Plum Pudding.

THE Aughton Pudding is not dead yet! It was a massive affair, containing a rich mixture of currants, raisins, figs, plums, almonds, sugar, lemon and spice, and was prepared every 21 years in the following manner:—

> *For ten days five fat bakers toiled*
> *A-kneading the flour into dough*
> *Which was in a ward boiler boiled*
> *Just a fortnight to make it enough . . .*

The delicacy measured 20ft. long, 6ft. thick and 18ft. in circumference, and all the surrounding villagers had to be called in to help in the eating of it.

The first Aughton Pudding was made early in the 19th century when two local basket-makers, R. and W. Lamb, bought a large boiler to enable them to peel the willows grown locally. A passing local who saw it declared, "By, that 'ud mak' a gert puddin'." And so the Aughton Pudding Feast was born. It was revived in 1971 after a lapse since the Feast of 1886.

Hornby and the Hero of Flodden.

WHEN Sir Edward Stanley, third son of the Earl of Derby, married Anne Harrington of Hornby, Hornby's ancient castle passed to the Stanleys. Sir Edward, a doughty warrior, went off to fight the Scots, slew their king and covered himself with glory on Flodden Field. For this he was created Lord Monteagle, Knight of the Garter, and in gratitude, and to fulfil a vow made before battle, he proceeded to add a chancel and an octagonal tower to St. Margaret's Church, Hornby. This was to be his last resting place, though the ballad tells us:

> *The beauteous tower and alter then appear'd*
> *But Stanley died before the Church was rear'd.*

He died about 1524 and, according to his wishes, his body was temporarily interred within the Priory Church of Hornby which then stood in an elevated situation near the Lune (on the site of Priory Farm). All religious houses were dissolved by order of Henry VIII, including Hornby Priory. There is no evidence that the remains of Flodden's hero were ever "exhumate and transferred" to the chancel of St. Margaret's, nor was a monument raised, as directed by his will; so the tradition maintains that somewhere, in the precincts of Priory Farm, the valiant hero lies sleeping still.

2

The Fylde

Hackensall Hall and its Boggarts.

LANDS IN Hackensall and Hambleton were granted to Geoffrey the Crossbowman by John, Count of Mortain (later the proud and foolish monarch of Magna Carta fame.) The Fleetwoods of Rossall took over in the 17th century and in 1656 Richard Fleetwood built the picturesque hall standing beside the Wyre banks, opposite Fleetwood. The initials of Richard and Anne Fleetwood appear over the doorway.

Hackensall has long been bothered with apparitions, including a spectral horse which was companionable and co-operative if it were well treated. It would get on with the farm work without being bidden so long as it could warm itself afterwards before a great roasting fire. If the kitchen went cold the horse would keep the household awake all night with its stampings and whinnyings.

Long ago, during major rebuilding, a bricked up cavity was discovered in one of the walls, containing one or two female human skeletons. The grim discovery gave credence to tales of ghostly presences and a priest had to be called in to exorcise the unhappy spirits. Exactly 100 years ago, "Atticus" (A. Hewitson of Preston) learned, during a visit, of another Wyreside sprite known as the "Hall Knocker" which got up to "all maks o' tricks." It would clean the shippons out—or it would turn awkward and dump manure in the buildings. The priest countered this perverse behaviour by "laying" the boggart beneath the threshold of an old house belonging to Stalmine Church.

The Kirkham Monster.

THERE WAS a commotion in 1643 at Kirkham, an ancient market town formerly engaged in the manufacture of sailcloth for the Royal Navy. Near Midsummer a hideous freak of nature, in the shape of a monstrous child, was born to a woman of popish persuasions who, during an altercation, had been heard to declare: "Rather than I shall become a Roundhead, or bear a Roundhead, I may bring forth a child without a head."

A headless child duly appeared, having "a face on the breast of it, two eyes near unto the place where the paps usually are, and a nose upon the chest and a mouth a little above the navel, and two ears, upon each shoulder one." To make assurance doubly sure, the body was disinterred and placed on view. A certificate signed by the Vicar, Edward Fleetwood, and Midwife Greenacre, widow of a previous incumbent, was exhibited in London and before the Commons so that "all the kingdom might see the hand of God to the comfort of His people and the terror of the wicked that deride and scorn them."

Lytham and St. Cuthbert's Cross.

A MODERN wayside cross fixed into an ancient base socket in a hedge bordering the cricket field in Church Road commemorates the Saint of Lindisfarne whose body, in its wooden sarcophagus, was carried by the monks in their flight from the Danes in the 9th century. The inscribed tablet tells us:

According to ancient tradition, the body of St. Cuthbert about the year 882 A.D. once rested here.

The cross was restored in 1912 by Lytham's blind Vicar, Canon Henry Beauchamp Hawkins, as a thank offering for recovery from serious illness. A church dedicated to St. Cuthbert has stood near the cross since the 12th century.

St. Cuthbert's body was carried over the Ribble estuary to Church-town, near Southport, progressed to Chester-le-Street and finally came to rest at Durham, where the Cathedral now covers the shrine. We are told that, years after his death, the tomb was opened and "whiles they opened his coffin they start at a wonder, they lookt for bones and found flesh, they expected a skeleton and saw an entire body with joynts flexible, his flesh so succulent that there wanted only heate . . . nay, his very funeral weeds were as fresh as if putrefaction had not dared to take him by the coat."

The Gory Head of Mowbreck Hall.

ANCIENTLY held by the Boteler (Butler) family whose ancestor came over with the Conqueror, Mowbreck Manor at Wesham, near Kirkham, passed to the Westby family who held it for more than 500 years until, heavily encumbered, it was sold to the Earl of Derby in 1893. William Westby of Mowbreck who was interred under his "pue" in the Mowbreck Chapel of Kirkham Church in 1557, left a son, John Westby, who succeeded, and daughters Elizabeth and Helen who married, respectively, George, brother of Cardinal William Allen of Rossall and one of the Haydocks of Cottam.

John Westby was steadfastly a Pope's man, prepared to defy Queen and all for the old religion. He abstained from church-going, as enjoined by the laws of the realm; he entertained the Queen's enemy, William Allen, and other priests, in his home; and he openly confessed these misdoings at the Bishop's Visitation at Lathom House in 1568. He was ordered to attend Divine Service on Sundays and to desist from harbouring priests.

Presently the missionary activities of the Jesuits, Campion and Parsons caused the laws to be tightened against Papists in a spirited attempt to reform "this so unbridled and bad a handful of England." The "rebellious minded" Westbys were crippled by fines, but their hospitable doors remained open to such notorious priests as Edmund Campion, Cardinal William Allen, Saint John Southworth of Samlesbury and Vivian Haydock, a widower priest with a late vocation, in connection with whom the Mowbreck legend had its origins.

Father Haydock, robed and about to say midnight Mass in the Mowbreck private chapel, stood before the altar at Hallowe'en, little suspecting that his priestly son, George, was about to be arrested in London—betrayed, it was thought, by a Fylde man called Hankinson. As midnight tolled, Father Haydock beheld the fearful sight of the severed, bloodstained head of his favourite son, George, hovering above the altar. The bleeding lips seemed to whisper: "Tristitia Vestra Vertetur in Gaudium." Father Haydock collapsed under the shock and lay temporarily bereft of speech. He died shortly afterwards and was buried in the chapel at Cottam Hall.

Many claimed to have seen the gory head in after years and few old Kirkhamites could ever be persuaded to venture up the tree-lined drive after darkness. Years ago, the Earl of Derby's agent occupied the hall, and a local milliner was requested to deliver a special order to the agent's wife late one evening. Bracing herself, the nervous milliner hurried between rustling bushes and sighing trees to the lonely hall. She managed to yank at the bell-pull before

Mowbreck Hall at Wesham, near Kirkham.

sliding into unconsciousness on the doorstep, where she was discovered by the butler. Something had appeared which had frightened her out of her wits though she would never divulge exactly what she had seen.

In the 1960s the hall was operated as a licensed country club and restaurant. All traces of the ancient chapel had been removed and the chamber was an ordinary bed-sitter, with no hint of gory heads, severed or otherwise. After the club closed, the vandals moved in and sadly marred this historic house, rebuilt in 1730, and once a hunting lodge of the Earls of Derby. Today there is a happier prospect of preservation.

Pilling—Skeletons in the Orchard.

THERE IS a farm on the great moss of Pilling which once had a sinister reputation. In the late 18th century, the Moores of Bone Hill Farm turned their isolated situation to good account. Young women "in trouble" were sent by their protectors to spend the waiting time in this supposedly sheltered harbour. But no-one in the district ever saw the babies being brought away and some of the women were never seen again. In time, it was rumoured that the skeleton of a baby could be found under every tree in the orchard. The existence of this old-time baby-farm is well authenticated. On the other hand, evidence of ancient British occupation in this region may account for the presence of bones.

Certainly, there was a stir in the district in 1824 when labourers, digging six feet below the surface, brought a piece of coarse woollen cloth of a yellow colour, enclosing the head of a woman with a great abundance of plaited auburn hair and a two-strand necklace of jet containing one amber bead. At the time it was attributed to the weird happenings at Bone Hill, less than a mile away. According to tradition, the head was ceremonially interred in Pilling Churchyard, and all the village attended with the exception of the Moores of Bone Hill. Archeologists now believe that this may have been a ritual bog-burial of the Iron Age. A report, at the time, described the peat as "undisturbed".

Poulton-le-Fylde and Teanlay Night.

INTO Victoria's reign, the night skies of the Fylde were annually illuminated by the Hallowe'en or Teanlay-Night bonfires when a circle of men with pitch forks lifted bundles of blazing straw on high. The object of this weird and ancient custom was to help departed friends who might be lingering halfway between heaven and hell. A field at Poulton where the ceremony had been enacted was always known as "Purgatory."

The Fylde Witch, Meg Shelton.

CRAFTY old Meg was reputed to be able to turn herself into inno-cent items of domestic equipment—which explains why she was never caught red-handed at her naughty tricks. Obviously, her broom-

stick was in good running order, for many widely-spread villages suffered from her depredations. Clever though she was supposed to be, Meg lived meagrely on a diet of seasoned boiled groats and stolen milk in a cottage at Cuckoo Hall, near Wesham.

When a cottage came vacant at Catforth she hankered after a house-move. She approached her landlord at Cottam and entered into a curious bargain. Meg would turn herself into a hare, Landlord Haydock would unloose his dogs and, if she gave them the slip and regained her cottage in safety, the Catforth cottage would be hers. The only stipulation was that the notorious black dog should not be freed. The hare bolted off at a smart pace, leaving its pursuers far behind. At length, the landlord could not resist the temptation to slip the black dog which raced off in time to nip the hare by the heel at the very door of the witch's cottage. Meg was left with a permanent limp, but she got her house at Catforth.

Another tale of Meg's mischief came from Singleton where the miller suspected her of stealing his corn. Night after night, he saw her cross the yard and enter the mill, but when he rushed in there was no Meg to be seen, and yet, next morning, he found he had been robbed. One night, determined to match guile with guile, he carefully counted the sacks of grain before Meg, as was her custom, crept into the mill. Rushing in, he counted again, and discovered that there was one sack more. Grinning with triumph, he seized a hay-fork and plunged it into each sack in turn until a scream of rage burst from the furious figure of Meg. While the miller stood transfixed, Meg snatched up a convenient broomstick and flew off into the night, never more to steal that miller's corn.

Laming cattle, turning milk sour and milking other people's cows were some of Meg's provoking habits. A farmer saw her, one day, jug in hand, flying over the hedge into his cow-pasture but when he arrived upon the scene the crafty old dame was quietly grazing her goose. The farmer was puzzled until he noticed some white liquid trickling off the bird's beak and realised that the greedy Meg had filled her jug to overflowing. He aimed a kick at the goose which shattered into fragments lying in a pool of spilt milk whilst Meg, with a wild scream, flew off over the hedge.

These are some of the legends, but Meg really lived. Margery Hilton of Catforth was found dead, crushed between a barrel and a wall, and was buried on 2nd May, 1705, by torchlight. Even then, the mischievous old madame would not rest quietly, but scratched her way to the surface so often that the priest from Cottam came to exorcise the place. Meg was re-interred, head downwards under the large boulder-stone beside the path in St. Anne's Churchyard, Woodplumpton.

St. Annes and the Legend of Kilgrimol.

THE NAME Kilgrimol means "the shingle-strewn corner of the sand-dunes". In the old days, natives of the St. Annes Old Links area claimed Kilgrimol was a church swallowed up by the sea. On New Year's Eve, or before a disaster, its bell could be heard tolling eerily under the waves. The Legend of the Lost Brother tells of Oswald the

Singleton mill, which had associations with Meg Shelton, the Fylde witch.

Gentle, "Prior of Kilgrimol" who survived the destruction of the great forest of Amounderness by a mighty inrush of the sea, but that phenomenon belongs to pre-history and the Fylde (green plain) has replaced the old forest.

Kilgrimol did exist, however, and was noted in maps and documents from the 12th century. It had a cemetery, too, near a boundary cross which named the now destroyed hamlet of Cross Slack. Tradition asserts that Kilgrimol was served by Culdees, members of an Irish order founded in the 8th century who became active in Scotland and northern England. Unlike the monasteries, the Culdees were not acquisitive but spent themselves in sacrificial service in the true spirit of "Companions or Servants of God."

Culdees were at York when King Athelstan sought a blessing at St. Peter's Church before his great battle in 937, and their ministrations to the sick, the poor and the lepers were impressive. After his victory, Athelstan gave Amounderness to the York Church and it is not impossible that one or two Culdees came here to serve the community. Much documentary evidence of that period was later destroyed by fire.

Kilgrimol was probably never more than a humble wood and shingle oratory which had decayed by the late 12th century. Nevertheless, its consecrated ground (under the tenth fairway) was used for the interment of local folk and washed-up bodies of sailors well into last century, and the shadows of long-forgotten graves are still visible from the air.

St. Michael's on Wyre and the Ghostly Major.

OLD St. Michael's Hall, on the Wyre was demolished more than a century ago. It bore the date 1590 on its studded door. To-day there is a farm of the same name near the site. The ghost of a former owner of the hall once shattered the serenity of the village by returning regularly to the place where he had spent most of his life. He was seen parading by the hall gates and heard clattering doors and furniture and jingling the cutlery. This veteran of the Civil Wars had seen the Royalists trounced by Cromwell at Preston in 1648 and routed by the Roundheads at Wigan Lane in 1651. In 1689, grey-haired and approaching the mid-sixties, he was promoted to the rank of Major in a trained band raised by Col. Richard Kirkby.

Perhaps it was this rumbustious and eventful life which prevented Major Longworth from sleeping quietly in his grave. The hauntings became so persistent that the combined powers of priest and parson were summoned to lay the troubled spirit which was commanded to rest "so long as the water flows down the hills and the ivy remains green." A hollow near the bridge was often pointed out as the place where the ghost of the restless Major was laid.

3

Between Ribble and Mersey

Bretherton—Carr House.

A QUAINT little bow-fronted toll-house on the Preston to Liverpool Road, at the corner of Carr House Lane, points the way to the Elder Doll Museum. Carr House was built in 1613 by two brothers, named Stones, for the occupation of a third engaged in sheep farming. A feature of the house is a rare cage newel around which the staircase was built. There is another at Swarthmoor Hall, near Ulverston, home of Margaret Fell who married George Fox, the founder of the Quaker movement.

It was at Carr House that Jeremiah Horrocks lodged during his brief curacy of Much Hoole Church in the late 1630s and in the first floor room above the porch he became the first man in history to predict and witness the transit of Venus with the aid of the most primitive equipment. He was 20 years old at the time, an ex-pupil of Emmanuel College, Cambridge, and a self-taught solitary student of astronomy. His treatise, "Venus sub Sole Visa" was barely completed when he died back home at Toxteth, near Liverpool, at the tender age of 21.

The homely and well-kept little country church of Much Hoole recalls with pride its associations with the celebrated astronomer. The date in the porch is 1628. The tower, sundial memorial, a stained glass window and marble tablet commemorating Jeremiah Horrocks were added later. (See Illustration on front cover)

Edward Kelley, Necromancer of Walton-le-Dale.

EDWARD KELLEY, an unscrupulous associate of Dr. Dee once practised his black arts in St. Leonard's Churchyard at Walton-le-Dale. Kelley, an Oxford scholar, was said to have lost his ears at Lancaster for a misdemeanour and afterwards wore an enveloping black cap to mask his disfigurement. After being discredited by the Doctor, Kelley bent his occult powers to the pursuit of money. Hearing that a Walton-le-dale worthy had died leaving considerable wealth in an undisclosed hiding place, Kelley and his new assistant,

Edward Kelley, the necromancer of Walton-le-Dale.

Paul Waring, repaired to the churchyard at midnight and opened the new grave and coffin.

Standing within a protective circle, the unholy pair, assisted by magic wand and consecrated torch, proceeded by ritualistic incantations to re-animate the corpse which rose from its narrow bed and stood before them. According to tradition, it divulged the whereabouts of the hidden money and uttered curious predictions which were later fulfilled. Kelley's impostures were hailed enthusiastically in Germany where he was knighted, but afterwards imprisoned. He escaped but fell through a window and died of his injuries in 1595. (See also Manchester, Dr. John Dee).

Haunted House of the Gradwells of Croston.

THE Gradwell family inherited Croston in 1571. They were devout Roman Catholics who suffered great persecution rather than abjure their faith. They maintained a chaplain in their home, and gave several sons to the priesthood. The first Gradwell here was William, whose initial W.G. appear on one of the gables. There are a hide beneath the hearth, signs of an escape which, some say, emerged inside Croston Church, and a stone cross in the garden commemorating a departed priest named Winckley.

For centuries the house was haunted by the Sarscowe Lady. She was never seen but was heard often enough. There was a delicate rustling of skirts as her dainty footsteps descended the fine oak staircase. The tale goes that a girl from Sarscowe Farm, half a mile distant, fell deeply in love with the chaplain at Gradwells. When he died of a fever her grief was inconsolable and she leapt to her death down the forty-foot well at the rear of the house.

Strangely enough, the Sarscowe Lady has not been heard in the thirteen years since the stone cross was moved from the orchard to its present site in the garden. Gradwells is famous to-day as the setting for the Royal Umpire Museum which has the finest collection of horse-drawn vehicles in the north, including Lord Derby's beautiful postillion carriage in which Queen Victoria used to travel, and antiquities of every conceivable kind, assembled by Mr. Martin Kevill.

Mawdesley—A Skull House and a Giant Poker.

THERE WAS a deal of good-natured chaff and leg-pulling when "Atticus" visited Mawdesley a century ago. "Th'awfullest place alive for chance childer," was the description, and half a barrow-load of bastardy orders were produced to prove it. Mawdesley Hall, half-timbered, dates back to 1625—a farmhouse now and somewhat decayed. A house at Lane End recalls the Catholic persecutions. A skull, kept in a box, in the attic once used as a chapel, is thought to be a relic of George Haydock, a young priest martyred in London in 1583. (See the legend of Mowbreck's Gory Head)

"Hell in Mawdesley," or "Hell Hob," can be traced to the old Black Bull Inn where an enormous poker, weighing sixteen pounds was once chained to the fireplace. "Hell" may be a corruption of "Hill," or may even refer to one "El-len" Mawdesley who once kept the house. It was a rough place in the old days, well known for wagers and fisticuffs: so much so, that they reckoned to sweep up a basketful of ears and nose-ends after the Saturday night combats—"and they made the finest manure in the world." There was once a great hob in the parlour and roysterers were fond of sitting upon it so that they could boast of having sat on the "Hob of Hell Fire."

The old hall nearby was supposed to be haunted by the ghost of an old lady. It was exorcised with incantations and the throwing of a bottle containing a candle into a pit of water. Landlord Rogerson of the Black Bull turned it to good advantage by placing a dirty bottle, containing a candle, on exhibition. Crowds flocked to see it and business was brisk until superstitious fears prompted the inn-keeper to throw the bottle into the pit, in the presence of witnesses.

Rufford and the Bard of Avon.

IT MAY BE no more than a fond hope, but a tradition persists that Shakespeare once performed at Rufford Old Hall, near Ormskirk. This picturesque half-timbered house, built in the late 15th century, with Carolean additions, was the home of the Hesketh family who acquired the manor by marriage during the 13th century. In 1949 a secret chamber was discovered at the hall, which belongs to the National Trust and also houses the Rufford Village Museum.

Evidence exists that a "William Shakeshaft" (another version of the name) was a youthful member of the Hesketh Company of Players who visited Rufford about 1585. This coincides with William's prudent absence from Stratford and the wife of his bosom after a high-spirited bout of deer-stealing from neighbouring parks, particularly that of Sir Thomas Lucy of Charlecote.

Lathom—The Eagle and Child and the Stanleys.

A QUAINT version of the legend in the history of "The Antient and Honourable House of Stanley" (1783) tells us that "Sir Thomas Latham lived in the reign of King Edward III and he and his Lady

being highly advanced in years without any other issue than Isabel (Lady Stanley): and he being desirous of male issue but despairing thereof by his own Lady, had a love intrigue with a young gentlewoman of his acquaintance, whom he kept concealed in a House of Retirement near him until she bore him a son, on the news whereof he was greatly rejoiced; but on due consideration, there still remained some articles of consequence to be adjusted for the future peace and quiet of Sir Thomas's mind ... the first whereof was, how and in what manner to publish the birth of his young son, and he not so much as suspected to be the real father of him. And next, how to amuse and secure his Lady from the pangs of a jealous mind and her motherly care of the young infant, in such manner that he might be nursed and brought up in his own house, free from all suspicion or uneasiness betwixt them."

Man-like, Sir Thomas resorted to a "pious cheat." arranging to have the babe deposited, not in the eagle's eyrie, which would have been dangerous, but on the ground under a nearby tree. Placing a servant on guard, the knight rushed back with his wife and family to view the "surprising Discovery he had by Accident made that Morning." The wise old dame pretended to fall for this tall story and suggested that they should adopt him for their son and heir "which was readily agreed to by his Father."

The child was christened Oskatell (his mother being one Mary Oskatell) and made heir to the estates and, in support of this supposed miracle, and to quell suspicions, Sir Thomas took for his device an eagle on the wing "turning her Head back, and looking in a sprightly manner as for something she had lost." But in the evening of his life the old man confessed that Sir Oskatell was only his natural son and all must go to Isabel, now Lady Stanley, and her descendants who, the account runs, "to distinguish or aggrandize themselves or in Contempt and Derision of their spurious Brother, took upon them the Eagle and Child for their Crest, in token of their Conquest over him."

Halsall and St. Cuthbert.

THERE IS a legend that when the shrine of St. Cuthbert was opened the head of King Oswald was found with the saint's remains. Five miles from Southport, at St. Cuthbert's Church, Halsall, a statue of the saint holding the king's head stands above the arch of the ancient renovated porch. Parts of this interesting church date back to Henry III.

Southport Upon Nile.

THERE IS a River Nile much nearer home than the one in Egypt— at Southport, in fact, though it is not particularly easy to locate

Relics at Formby. Left: The wooden cross. Right: The Godstone.

until it trickles forth to meet the tide on Birkdale sands. A light-hearted legend tells about the naming of this man-made water-course flowing between sand-dunes before modern Southport came into being. The resort's founder, William Sutton, moved to South Hawes in 1798, into a new house which, at a convivial house-warming, was christened The Duke's Folly. At the same time, the embryo village was named South Port in a traditional bottle-smashing ceremony. Nelson's famous Nile victory occurred in the same year and "The Duke" bestowed that name on the inconspicuous water-way in honour of England's naval hero—or so the story goes!

Formby—The Godstone.

UNDER THE trees in a corner of St. Luke's Churchyard, Formby is a curious egg-shaped stone marked with a Calvary cross surmounted by a circle, In pre-Christian times it was the custom to carry a corpse three times round the God stone in order to contain the spirit of the departed and prevent it from coming back to haunt the relatives. One theory is that the stone was originally placed here by pagan settlers and that the Christian symbols were added later by missionaries who came to convert them. This was an instance of applied psychology and it would help to effect the transition. (The practice of carrying the corpse three times round the churchyard was witnessed by an English traveller to Holland a few years ago).

Formby has other interesting relics in the village stocks, set up for

Speke Hall, near Liverpool, a magnificent "magpie" mansion.

safety in the churchyard, and the tall old village cross, now encased in zinc for presevation, which gazes down on the tombs of the Formbys of Formby. From this ancient family sprang the giant, Richard Formby, fully seven feet in height and armour-bearer to the king. His memorial slab was damaged by fire at York Minster in 1829 and was brought back to lie on the porch floor at St. Luke's. Translated, the Latin inscription reads:

Here lies Richard Formby formerly armour bearer
of our Lord and King, who died on the 22nd Day
of the month of September in the year of our Lord
1407. Upon whose soul may God have mercy.

Speke Hall and the White Lady.

NOWHERE IN Lancashire better deserves its apparition than Speke Hall, home of the Norreys or Norris family from the 14th century. This magnificent "magpie" mansion, grouped round a courtyard where Adam and Eve flourish (two yew trees said to be 500 years old), and situated close to the banks of Mersey, was the coastal clearing centre for Roman Catholic priests who came from the Continent to work at great peril in the country.

The manor house consisted originally of a single large hall to which extensions were added between 1490 and 1598. Edward

Norris completed the north frontage bearing the inscription: "This worke, 25 yds long, was wholly built by Edw:N:Esq: ano 1598," and it was either Edward or his father William who constructed a veritable rabbit warren of hides, runs, look-outs, listening holes, secret stairs and trapdoors. A moat at the front afforded protection from the sudden swoops of Government agents, and the Mersey where the Norris family moored their boats, provided a safe get-away at the rear. Priests were coming and going like commercial travellers but, so far as is known, none was ever arrested at Speke. Nor were the Norrises arrested though heavy fines for recusancy were imposed from time to time. It was hinted that a Norris could not be touched, "through fear of his greatness."

Hints of ghostly apparitions would explain away any suspicious noises emerging from the priest's room and curb the curiosity of domestic servants. Yet it is the Tapestry Room which is said to be haunted. The last male Norris died in 1731. The estate came to Mary Norris who, at the age of 36, contracted a disastrous marriage with Lord Sidney Beauclerk ("Worthless Sidney"), younger son of the Duke of St. Albans and descendant of Charles II and Nell Gwynn. Their son's gambling excesses led to the sale of the property in 1797. Traditionally, it was a Beauclerk lady who, fresh from childbed and facing financial ruin through her husband's reckless ways, threw her child from the Tapestry room window into the moat. She ran down to the Great Hall and took her own life and her unhappy shade still hovers about Speke Hall.

Hale and the Lancashire Giant.

IN 1844, Hale was described by Mrs. Carlyle as the "beautifullest village in all England," and few would quarrel with that statement today. Hale has plenty of thatch and whitewash to charm the eye, and bright cottage gardens, and farmsteads beyond with cornfields sweeping down to Mersey water, three miles wide at this point. The village inn is named after the "Childe of Hale," and in St. Mary's churchyard railings surround the enormous grave of John Middleton, the village giant.

He was born in 1578 and lived with his widowed mother in a thatched cottage still to be seen. The only legends are about the manner of his growing to the astonishing height of 9ft. 3ins. Some said it happened overnight, as a result of magic. Others said he fell asleep in a sandy hollow, woke up to find his clothes burst asunder and tackled and threw an angry bull on the way home. Maybe he was "strong i'th arm and weak i'th heyd." We are not enlightened on that point.

We do know that in 1617 Sir Gilbert Ireland of Hale Hall and a few friends amused themselves by taking the Childe down to London to challenge the King's champion. But first they accoutred him

John Middleton, the "Childe of Hale," who grew to a height of 9 ft. 3 in.

magnificently in the fashion of the time, with ruffs, striped doublet, embroidered girdle, plush breeches, green stockings, stylish shoes with red heels and tie-ribbons and a fine sword suspended on an embroidered shoulder belt. A plumed hat topped this outlandish spectacle of a modish gentleman almost twice the normal size. We are not told how he was conveyed to the capital but his journey down must have excited great comment.

James I was not amused when the Lancashire challenger beat the champion hollow and dislocated his thumb. The "Childe" was given £20 and dismissed, and on the way home stayed awhile at Brazenose College, Oxford, where he was a welcome curiosity, and where his life-size portrait was painted. The zenith of his strange career had been reached, and nothing remained but to return home to the cottage which he had to enter on his hands and knees and where he could stand erect only under the ridge where the ceiling had been cut away. So doing, one day, he terrified two burglars who had climbed upon an outhouse roof and were about to break in through the gable-end window. They thought it was Old Nick himself and bolted all the way to the banks of the Mersey.

John Middleton died in 1623 and for years his bones were kept at Hale Hall before being buried. Later, doubts arose about the actual size of the "Childe" whose remains were exhumed. Examination proved the height of 9ft. 3ins. The thighbone was as long as a normal man's whole leg. The hand was 17ins long from carpus to finger-tip and the palm was 8½ins across.

Robin Hood of Upholland

GEORGE LYONS emulated Sherwood's romantic outlaw. Like Robin Hood, it was his pleasure to steal from the rich and give to the poor but he danced at the rope's end when he was caught making off with newly baked bread from the Owl Inn, Upholland, in memory of which the "Robber's Grave" is still pointed out at the top end of the hillside burial ground.

4   From Preston to the Fells

Goosnargh and the Chingle Hall Ghost

OFF THE ROAD from Broughton to Goosnargh lies a small cruciform manor house, still partially moated, which Adam de Singleton first built in the 13th century, using massive curved timbers hauled from Ribble wrecks more than 700 years ago. The original sturdy front door still bears the heavy "Y" knocker, rare in this country. Thatch has given way to slates and a stone bridge has replaced the original drawbridge. Nevertheless, Chingle Hall preserves its air of antiquity, largely due to the sensitive restoration work undertaken by the present owner.

The Wall family, relatives of the de Singletons, succeeded to the estate in 1585, at which time the authorities were stepping up the persecution of Roman Catholics. Chingle Hall became an active Mass centre, with a tiny signal window in the porch where a lighted candle would indicate when the Mass was about to be celebrated. The faithful would steal over the fields and slip into the house undetected. A few years ago, the old chapel was located when plaster was accidentally dislodged revealing a wooden cross recessed into the wall of a room where a hide in the hearth was already known. To celebrate the event, a historic meeting between the Roman Catholic Archbishop Heenan of Liverpool and the Protestant Bishop Dr. Hoskyns-Abrahall of Lancaster took place at the Hall on 6th April, 1962.

A false wall with a hide in the priest's room upstairs had also been discovered, but it was only in spring, 1971, when fire threatened, that two further hides and an escape route came to light. Nevertheless, Chingle Hall has many secrets yet, and one may concern St. John Wall who was born in the house in 1620. He joined the Franciscan Order in 1651 and, after years of missionary work in the Midlands, was hanged, drawn and quartered at Worcester in 1679. There is a tradition that his head is hidden somewhere on the premises—in the cellars, perhaps, which have not yet been found though they appear on the original 13th century plans.

A spiritualist has stated that valuable documents are also to be found and, until that day, the haunting will continue. The gh)st of a male cloaked figure is often seen in the birth-chamber of St. John Wall and the door has an unnerving habit of opening and closing. The figure has been seen by many, crossing the bridge, entering the porch and ascending the stairs, and manifesting its presence by rappings and tappings, flowers shaking in their vases, pictures dancing on the wall and the occasional dislodgement of objects. Mercifully, the Chingle ghost seems harmless and causes no alarm to the occupants.

Our Lady's Well, Fernyhalgh.

WELL KNOWN to Roman Catholic pilgrims and set in one of Lancashire's beauty spots, though only four miles from Preston, the Ladywell at Fernyhalgh had a legend as romantic as its setting. Centuries ago, a pious and wealthy Irish merchant encountered a fearful storm in the Irish Sea and vowed to perform some outstanding deed of devotion if his life were spared. Landing safely in Lancashire, he was commanded in a vision to seek a place called Fernyhalgh where a spring would be found beneath a crab-tree bearing fruit without cores. In that place he must erect a chapel.

For a long time he sought vainly. Then, lodging one night near Preston, he overheard the milkmaid apologising for her delayed return. A cow had strayed from the common and she had pursued it as far as Fernyhalgh. Greatly excited, he was taken to that place in the morning and duly found the crab tree and the well—close beside which was an image of the Virgin Mary. The merchant fulfilled his promise and erected the chapel which was dedicated to the Virgin Mother of God. The spring was ever afterwards called the Ladywell. Countryfolk, in the old days, attributed miraculous healing powers to its waters.

Whittingham and the Old Rib.

UP Halfpenny Lane, Whittingham, there is a charming 17th century stone dwelling once known as Dun Cow Rib Farm. It has mullion windows, dripstones, studded door and lintel dated 1616, above which the curious passer-by will notice a puzzling bow-shaped object. This is the famous Old Rib taken from a great duncow, long ago, when prolonged drought brought hardship to Lancashire. The heatwave persisted, drying up streams, browning the fields, ruining crops and slimming the cattle.

The country area around Longridge was particularly hard hit and to fend off complete starvation a great dun cow was sent roaming as far as Grimsargh and Goosnargh so that desperate housewives could milk her when needful. The beneficent beast gave freely of her

Top: The haunted Chingle
Hall, near Goosnargh.

Right: Our Lady's Well
Fernyhalgh.

Old Rib Farm, Whittingham.

bounty until an evil old crone, who had delighted in the distress of her neighbours, decided to cut off this lifegiving stream. Early one morning, the Longridge witch tracked the dun cow to its pasturage and proceeded to draw milk into a sieve which, of course, never filled. At length, the poor animal fell utterly exhausted and expired as the next customers appeared on the scene.

The skeleton of the giant cow was revered by many generations and one of her ribs was mounted over the door of Old Rib Farm. A story goes that the rib was once removed and hidden in Charnley Brook by a practical joker who afterwards was beset by so many misfortunes that he retrieved the relic and returned it to its old position.

Longridge and the Written Stone.

LEAVE Longridge by the Dog Inn along the road to Dilworth and, past the reservoir, watch out for an inconspicuous cross-lane with a "Public Footpath" notice. This is Written Stone Lane, once the old Roman highway from Ribchester to Lancaster. The Written

THE WRITTEN STONE.

Stone is a great slab, measuring 8ft. by 2ft. and 18ins. deep, set into an embankment beneath a holly hedge, and bearing a remarkably clear message, after all these years:

> *Ravffe: Radcliffe: Laid: This*
> *Stone to Lye: For: Ever: A.D. 1655.*

Why the stone was laid remains a mystery. One story is that a murder was committed here and the victim's ghost plagued the Radcliffe family in the farmhouse nearby. Parish registers show that several of Ralph's family died shortly before the stone was carved, by his order, perhaps in the hope of quietening the restless spirit. Travellers spoke of queer goings-on up that lane, of bumpings and screechings, scratchings and pinchings, of cloaks tweaked and hats plucked off, and it was all put down to the "boggarts."

After the Radcliffes' time, a new tenant sized up the great slab and decided it would make an excellent buttery stone for the dairy, but moving it took six horses and many helpers, caused much personal injury and destroyed the peace of the household. The stone seemed bedevilled; nothing would remain safely upon it, neither pot, pan, nor kettle. Everything tilted and spilled and, what with shakings and clatterings through the night, and sleep destroyed, the farmer began to regret the move. "Id mun goo back," he cried, "and happen boggart'll goo back wi' it." The horses were re-summoned for the uphill journey but, strangely enough, only one was required. The Written Stone seemed anxious to get back beneath the holly hedge, where it can be seen to this day.

There are plenty of queer tales about Written Stone Lane. One concerns the local doctor who, when driving past the stone after a night call, had to cope with a hysterical horse. It reared and screamed and plunged off at a headlong gallop, defying all attempts to control it, and halted two miles away, sweating, foam-flecked and covered in blood. The same doctor, suitably fortified at a nearby inn, ventured a second encounter with the boggart. He rode boldly up to the stone and issued a challenge, whereupon a shapeless mass materialised, seized him, plucked him from the saddle and almost squeezed the breath from his body. He was descried by his friends, galloping madly away from the stone.

Inglewhite—St. Ann's Well.

PILGRIMS came in droves long ago to drink and bathe themselves in the healing waters of St. Ann's Well, which is sited in a field on Longley Hall estate, Inglewhite. There is not much to be seen today—a spring and a swampy place churned up by cattle—but

during last century the well. shaped like a horse-shoe and measuring 9ft. by 7½ft. had steps leading to water almost a yard deep. There was an inscribed stone tablet with letters 3½ inches h gh. A dissertation of 1740 mentions Inglewhite Spa as being "a strong sulphur and chalybeate water but purges not except drunk with salts." An earlier work (1700) asserts that the water had "a sulphureous smell as strong as that near Harrogate . . . but contains little or no salt, which is the reason that it is not purgative."

The Bleasdale Circle.

THE SPECTACULAR discovery of the Bleasdale Circle was made during excavations on land belonging to Fairsnape Farm at the end of last century. Cinerary urns, containing human ashes, were discovered two feet below ground. The pottery was identified by archaeologists as belonging to the Middle Bronze Age (2,500-750 B.C.) The Circle was probably connected with some primitive form of worship in which the rising sun was part of the ritual.

The belief that the Midsummer sun rises over a cleft in Fairsnape Fell when viewed from the circle has no foundation. You may try it —if you have a mind to tramp in the footsteps of the Bronze Age natives who once roamed and hunted and tended their beasts there, and may even have had a stockaded settlement nearby. Or you may prefer to visit the Harris Museum, Preston, where the antiquities are lodged.

5

The Ribble Valley

The Cuerdale Hoard.

THERE WAS great excitement in 1840 when a gang of workmen, excavating earth from the Ribble banks (not far from the motorway bridge beyond Ha'penny Broo, out of Preston) uncovered a leaden chest containing 10,000 silver coins, almost 1,000 ounces of silver ingots of various sizes, and a collection of ornaments and armlets. Most of the coins were Danish and had been minted at York before 928, though many were from the mints of Alfred the Great, Edward the Elder, and others.

There have been many romantic theories about the treasure. It may have been hidden by the Danes in flight before Edward the Elder in 911; it may have been loot, abandoned by pirates; it may even have been an army pay chest, hastily jettisoned after the battle of Brunanburgh in 937 when King Athelstan defeated a massed coalition of Irish, Welsh, Danes, Scots and Northumbrians, and welded the whole of England into one kingdom. The cache was declared to be Treasure Trove and was dispersed to various museums, though many of the coins had subsequently wandered "by some means or other." An inscribed stone indicates the SITE OF THE CUERDALE HOARD 15TH MAY 1840.

Samlesbury and the Witch's Grave.

THERE ARE several stories to account for the cracked grave-slab, clamped by iron bars, in the churchyard of St. Leonard the Less, Samlesbury. If it was the resting place of a witch who would keep getting out, certainly there were enough reputed "witches" in the locality, several of whom stood trial in the 17th century. An alternative version relates to a nagging wife who repeatedly returned to torment her remarried husband.

In desperation, it was said, he had the slab replaced and firmly anchored by the bars which are visible through the crack, and lived in peace ever after. There are even suggestions that the bars were a precaution against the "Resurrection Men" who once were active

Samlesbury Old Hall and its white apparition.

conveniently near to medical colleges, but Samlesbury was an un-
likely place for their activities. The damage can probably be attributed to an act of irreverent vandalism.

Samlesbury Old Hall and the White Lady.

MANY CLAIM TO have seen the White Lady of Samlesbury who,
legend insists, was Dorothy, daughter of Sir John Southworth, a
16th century knight, an ardent Catholic and High Sheriff of the
County Palatine. This tough, mettlesome gentleman fought with
equal vigour in battlefield and law court, plotted to rescue Mary
Queen of Scots and to overthrow the Church of England, resisting
all efforts to convert him though, time and again, arrested and confined. The Southworths had lived since 1325 in the picturesque black
and white manor house, then deeply embosomed in woodland.

The story goes that Sir John's daughter Dorothy fell deeply in
love with a Protestant neighbour, one of the de Hoghtons, thus
arousing her father's implacable anger. His opposition only deepened
the tender devotion of the lovers, who met by stealth and plotted an
elopement. Unfortunately, their plans were overheard by Dorothy's
brother, who surprised the luckless pair at their secret rendezvous
and slew the young man and his male companion, burying their
bodies deep in the woodland. Dorothy never recovered from the

horror of that night and languished her grief-stricken days in some far off convent, dying with her lover's name on her lips. The discovery of two human skeletons in the moat when the road was carved through the woods in 1826 gives some credence to the tale.

Though the pale shade of Dorothy often glides across the lawns and through the house, the Southworth pedigree does not corroborate her existence. Yet Samlesbury with its Roman Catholic connections, its secret rooms and cavities, its harbouring of priests and its blood-splashed floorboards, has earned the right to claim a gentle apparition.

Pleasington Old Hall and a Real Dorothy.

THE CONFUSION surrounding the previous story turns our attention to Dorothy Winckley of Pleasington Old Hall, a small moated manor house some three miles from Samlesbury. About the time of John Southworth this Dorothy married, first a Southworth, then a de Hoghton, and finally Thomas Ainsworth, a lawyer, whose family later became Protestants. All the ingredients are there for the "Dorothy" legend. Pleasington Old Hall, which bears the date 1587, has a Mass cupboard and evidence of hides. The front portion is now a farmhouse and the rear is decayed.

Samlesbury—Sykes Lumb Boggart and Ghost.

BEFORE THE airfield wiped away several old farms at Samlesbury and banished the fairies, the centuries-old farmhouse of Sykes Lumb stood in a secluded spot beside Mellor Brook, not far from Samlesbury Old Hall. A boggart lived there who was amiable and helpful— so long as he was accorded due respect. A slighting word by family or servants roused him to anger and he would revenge himself by hurling crockery, unloosing beasts, tampering with carts and plucking off bedclothes so that sleep was lost in nights of prolonged terror. Then he would fly off to a beam in the barn and hug himself with glee.

The ghost at Sykes Lumb Farm was a hang-over from the disturbed times of the Wars of the Roses when the childless Sykes couple, fearful of being robbed, placed their savings in jars and buried them under the apple tree in the orchard. By the time Henry VII was peacefully enthroned, old man Sykes had died and his penny-pinching widow alone possessed the secret. Suddenly, she died and the knowledge accompanied her to the grave. Desultory digs by hopeful relatives revealed nothing, the jars remained entombed and the ghost of the frustrated Sykes wife haunted the farmstead. Many sighted the wrinkled and bent old dame crossing the Lumb with her crooked stick and old-fashioned garments, but no one summoned up courage to address her: the Lumb became a place to avoid after dark.

Long after the Sykes were gone and forgotten, the farm tenant was returning home after an evening of merriment when he encountered the old woman and, emboldened by liquor, dared to enquire the reason for her visits. Soundlessly, she drifted before him, drawing him to the stump of an old apple tree, and pointing to the ground beneath it. Spades were brought out, digging commenced and, at the bottom of a deep trench, the jars were discovered. With a last smile of ineffable satisfaction, the ghost of the Sykes wife faded before the eyes of the diggers, and never more was seen.

Whalley and the Catterall Monumental Brass.

Of yo charyte pray for the sowllys of Raffe Catterall esquyer and Elizabeth hys wyfe whyche bodies lyeth before thys pellor and for all ther Chylder sowlys whyche Rafe descesyd the xxvi day of december y yere of o'Lord God M'CCCCC'XV on whose sowlys JHU have mercy amen.

THE BRASS is said to have been unearthed at St. Helen's Churchyard, Churchtown, and kept for some time at Catterall House nearby before being returned to Whalley. A quick count reveals nine sons and eleven daughters - a rare quiverful in any age!

Stonyhurst and the Last of the Shireburnes.

RICHARD FRANCIS, last of the Shireburne males, died in 1702 at the age of eight years, supposedly after eating yew berries whilst lost in his father's maze. Sir Nicholas had spent a lifetime embellishing the estate to hand on to his heirs. The legend lacks credibility, however, considering that the labyrinth was incomplete at that time and that there are no yew berries in June. Oliver Cromwel! slept at Stonyhurst, a Royalist household, on his way to the Battle of Preston in 1648 but, fearing assassination, he spent the night on a dining table in the great hall with his sword at the ready.

It stands in the College Refectory to-day, 'still stinking of Old Noll", and an object of great interest. Stonyhurst passed through the female line to the Welds of Lulworth Castle, Dorset. In 1794 Thomas Weld, a former pupil of the Roman Catholic College at Liege, offered Stonyhurst to the priests and masters put to flight by the French Revolution.

Clitheroe

RIBBLESDALE is a happy hunting ground for students of legend and folk-lore. The castle rock heaves above Clitheroe town, the keep has a Devil's Window made by the Evil One tossing rocks from the Nick o' Pendle, and there are memories of Old Noll in Cromwell's Cave. The Devil was partial to Clitheroe. by all accounts, stalking the streets. waylaying good Christians with the offer of three wishes for a soul, and acting like a first-class nuisance until bested by the astute Clitheronians. Then, with a swish of his tail, he vanished at Hell Hole Bridge.

Peg o' Nell's Well.

IN A MEADOW by the river at Waddow Hall, a headless statue stands innocently beside a springlet, though it is reputed to claim a human life every seven years. Possibly it came from a niche in some Roman Catholic institution for, traditionally, it is the figure of Saint Margaret. During the bitter religious quarrels, her new owners reduced her name to Peg, and Peg o'th'Well, as she was known, became a most convenient peg on which to hang all domestic disasters. Accidents, storms or broken bones were all put down to "Peggy's work." One time, a Puritan preacher was expected at the hall. He was overtaken by a freshet in the river while crossing Brungerly Hipping Stones (the very place where Henry VI was captured by the Talbots of Bashall in 1464). The worried Mistress Starkie ordered a search and the servants returned with the half-drowned divine.

Declaring that this was Peg at her old tricks, the good lady rushed down to the statue and chopped off its head with an axe. The head lay for years in a gloomy lumber room at the top of the house, until a servant, who laughed at such superstitious nonsense, cleaned it up and brought it down to the pantry.

"Does she ever plague you now?" she was asked.

"No. There is not a better girl in all the parish. I fear she was much slandered," was the cheerful reply.

The legend of the Dule upon Dun.

Dule upon Dun.

ON THE ROAD from Clitheroe to Waddington, a painted sign depicting the Devil upon a dun horse used to hang outside an ancient public house. It was the home of an ale-swilling tailor whose feckless ways had reduced him to poverty. Whilst drinking with companions in their favourite bar parlour one night, he was joined by a plausible stranger (the Devil in disguise) who beguiled him with promises of riches upon reciting a magical incantation. Next morning, when his wife went out gossiping, the tailor resolved to put it to the test. Instantly, the Devil appeared, asking his pleasure.

The tailor was alarmed, but the visitor was impatient to settle the matter. It was arranged that the first three wishes uttered by either the tailor or his wife would be granted and, in exchange, the tailor's soul would be collected in twenty years' time. The tempter departed and the goodwife returned, grumbling that there was only oatcake to put on the table. Now, if only there were a good backstone! . . . the backstone appeared in a flash. The tailor was furious at this waste of a good wish and hoped it would smash to fragments . . . which it did!

With two precious wishes wasted, he confessed the whole business to his wife and she begged him to consult the Abbot of Whalley, which he dared not, for fear of being charged with Devil-dealing.

The third wish was as carelessly spent—an extra collop of bacon or a can of hot water for shaving—and the tailor realised that he was doomed. In desperation, he consulted the Hermit of Pendle who urged him to reform, work hard and put his trust in God.

By so doing he prospered and made good but twenty years passed, the appointed day arrived and his Satanic Majesty appeared, in a clap of thunder, to claim his bond. Bravely, the tailor faced the visitor. calling him a cheat and a trickster, casting doubt on his alleged powers and pouring scorn on the promises which had done no whit of good. The Devil threw a tantrum of outraged pride and offered yet one more wish to prove his ability.

At that moment, the tailor happened to espy a dun horse grazing along the hedgerows. "I Wish thou wert galloping into Hell upon yonder dun horse, never to return to earth to plague poor mortals," cried he. With a yell that could be heard in far off Colne, the Devil upon the dun horse galloped off across the wide heavens, outwitted by this sturdy son of Lancashire. Many came to visit the scene and to congratulate the tailor who further prospered by turning his home into an alehouse which flourished for centuries.

Downham and the Curse of the Asshetons.

DOWNHAM has been described as the prettiest village in Lancashire and certainly it lacks nothing that man and nature can contrive for the refreshment of town-jaded eyes—hall and ancient church tower, village green, handloom weavers' houses and bonny stone cottages sweeping up from the stream below, with the green mass of Pendle brooding beyond. The Asshetons came to Downham in 1558 and their hall was ancient then. Nowadays, it masquerades behind a Georgian facade.

By tradition, there is an ancient curse on the Asshetons. If one steps upon the grave of Abbot Paslew of Whalley Abbey, he is supposed to die within the year. Paslew, the last Abbot of Whalley, was executed at Lancaster in 1537 for supporting the pilgrimage of Grace. Legend will insist that, after his conviction, he was brought back to Whalley and hanged at the monastery gates, but there is no foundation for this claim. Nor is it likely that the gravestone in Whalley Churchyard marks the last resting place of the fated Abbot.

6

Pendle Country and the North-East

Pendle Legends.

PENDLE is the place for superstitions and secrets. There was gold found here once, and rubies and silver and lead. The ancient Britons knew this brooding hill, and the Romans who struggled to the summit to worship their gods. Folk still climb it to watch mid-summer sunrise and youngsters, dressed as witches, go on pony-back at Hallowe'en.

Pendle has a temper, too. From some elaborate cave system, or subterranean reservoir, a great torrent of water has poured forth from time to time. Camden mentions it happening about 1580 and "the damage it lately did in the country below." In 1669, a water burst "from the butt-end of Pendle" made a breast a yard high, overwhelmed Worston village two miles away and ruptured Pendle in five or six places. Mearley Clough and Brast Clough wear their scars still.

Quakers came to Pendle, following in the footsteps of their founder George Fox who, in 1652, and not long out of Derby gaol on a charge of blasphemy, "was moved of the Lord to go to the top of it; which I did, with much ado." From this fine look-out, George had his clear vision of a great people waiting to be enlightened and gathered in. His mission was to take him across the Atlantic.

The 17th century witches of Pendle Forest still stir the imagination though the "forest" was only a chase, reserved for the king's pleasure and the "witches" were a poor rabble of depraved and deluded peasants. A pair of decrepit beldams, Demdike and Chattox, headed the two rival clans. Demdike (Elizabeth Southern) of Malkin Tower lived in squalor with her graceless brood—daughter Elizabeth Device and grandchildren, Alison, James and Jennet. Chattox (Anne Whittle) sojourned with her daughters, Anne Redfearn and Bessie Whittle, in a cottage close by. All subsisted by begging and by extracting doles from neighbours by threat of witchcraft.

In 1612, Bessie Whittle touched off a conflagration, destined to consume the two families and their associates, by breaking into Malkin Tower and stealing oatmeal and articles of clothing which she recklessly wore to church the following Sunday. Within hours

Roughlee Hall, once the home of Alice Nutter, one of the Pendle witches.

Demdike's granddaughter, Alison, lodged a complaint with the magistrate at Read. Bessie counter-charged Alison with witchcraft. Alison hurled similar accusations at the whole Chattox circle and thus, tragically and relentlessly, the quarrelling neighbours delivered themselves into the hands of the hangman. Mr. Nowell, J.P., flushed out a whole tribe of supposed witches who were conveyed to Lancaster and slung into the castle dungeons.

Nine witches from Pendle were tried and found guilty, and ten from Samlesbury and elsewhere shared the same fate. Old Mother Demdike was fortunate—she died before trial. The two anti-heroines of the court hearing were the mischievous young Jennet Device who stood upon a court room table and cheerfully swore away the lives of her nearest and dearest; and Grace Sowerbutts of Samlesbury, who was dismissed as "an impudent wench delivering a strangely devised accusation." The whole scene was redolent of the witch-hunting hysteria of the times and one wonders equally at the credulity of the justices and the damning and fanciful confessions of the victims, as related by Thomas Potts, Clerk to the Justices, in his "Wonderfvll Discoverie of Witches in the Cvntie of Lancaster."

Rising enigmatically from this obscene tragedy is the lone figure of Alice Nutter of Roughlee. The hall of the Nutters stands yet divided into cottages and occupied to this day. Mistress Nutter was a widow of gentle birth, blessed with riches and "children of good hope." How she came to be associated with the pitiful peasant, of Pendle and their hallucinatory ramblings is anybody's guess.

She steadfastly denied the charge of murder by witchcraft and went impenitent to the scaffold, in 1612.

In 1633, another round-up of so-called witches in Pendle, was based on the evidence of a precocious eleven-year-old, Edmund Robinson of Wheatley Lane. It is gratifying to note that the imp of the previous trial, Jennet Device, was amongst the suspects bundled off up to Lancaster. Seventeen were found guilty, some were exhibited in London's Fleet Prison, most were reprieved, and what happened to the rest is not recorded. Times had changed. James I was dead and belief in witchcraft, with occasional relapses, was on the decline. The boy Robinson recanted under examination in London, was separated from his father and uncle who had set him up as a witch-detector, and returned to Wheatley Lane to live out his life as "Ned o' Roughs."

The Boggart of Hollin Hey Clough, Near Burnley.

THE RIVER BRUN flows not far from Towneley Hall, Burnley, and the people of that area were once tormented by a mischievous boggart who would station himself at the bridge to waylay travellers. The natives would make a long detour to avoid him and at last, in exasperation, they begged the Towneley priest to exorcise the sprite with bell, book and candle. It was a tough assignment. The boggart refused to be laid until he had extracted the promise that, on one day in every year, he could claim the first creature to cross over the bridge. On that condition he would refrain from bothering honest folks "as long as a green leaf grows in the clough."

Every year, the inhabitants kept their side of the bargain by giving the boggart a barnyard rooster and he, in turn, kept his. One year, however, two farmhands noticed a stranger approaching the bridge at daybreak and they raced to warn him of the danger, but arrived too late. The wayfarer had disappeared with a wild scream and a splash. Afterwards, the clough-folk planted plenty of evergreen holly bushes to keep the boggart under control and the name of the place became known as Hollin Hey Clough.

Towneley Hall and the Ghost of Sir John.

IF Speke Hall was the coastal base for priests, Towneley Hall, Burnley, was the inland centre of Catholic life in Northern England. The Towneleys settled here in the 13th century. Their impressive hall, embattled and moated, was originally built in quadrangular form round a courtyard, having stout walls for defence and several priest-hides, cunningly constructed, including a 16ft. square chamber, soundproofed with clay and rushes. Several priests could be housed simultaneously at Towneley—reason enough to invent convenient 'ghosts.'

Above: Towneley Hall, Burnley. Opposite: The great fireplace of Wycoller Hall, near Colne.

Nevertheless, the ghost of Towneley appears to have been that of Sir John Towneley who built the hall's domestic chapel and was Sheriff of Lancashire during Henry VII's reign. He caused a rumpus early in the 16th century by illegally enclosing 200 acres of common land which divided his Hapton and Towneley estates. The poor folk of Horelaw and Hollinhey, who had anciently enjoyed their rights of common, were aggrieved when given notice to quit and muttered darkly against the land-hungry knight, asserting that they had "as much right to their bits of land as John Towneley had to his acres." By quittance-day, not a family had moved. Three nights later, men at arms escorted in a band of ruffians who set about evicting the cottagers and smashing up their homesteads. No one was spared, not even an elderly widow-woman whose tears still flowed for the recent loss of her husband. She died within days of shock and grief.

It is said that Sir John's determination to "lay in" the peasants' land brought him nothing but remorse. He was constantly heard muttering to himself and died a tormented man, crying out at the end: "Lay out, lay out." The dispossessed peasants believed that his restless spirit wandered about the hall and over the disputed acres, crying most piteously:!

> *Be warned!. Lay out!. Lay out!. Be warned!.*
> *Around Horelaw and Hollinhey Clough*
> *To her children give back the widow's cot*
> *For you and yours there's still enough.*

Wycoller and the Spectral Horseman.

ALMOST deserted now, and not far from Colne, the bonny hamlet of Wycoller is well worth a visit. Proud even in decay, some of its stone houses go back to the early 16th century. A twin-arched pack-horse bridge spans the stream which separates the community from the ruins of Wycoller Hall and a slab footbridge a little upstream has done service since the 12th century. Wycoller was once a flourishing community of several hundred souls engaged in spinning and weaving. Year round, it is a sweet spot, particularly in spring-time, but see it in winter under a blanket of fresh snow, with the sky reddened by the sinking afternoon sun, and the memory will remain for ever of this place beloved of the Brontes. Charlotte took Wycoller Hall, which was almost entire in her day, as the inspiration for Ferndean Manor in "Jane Eyre." Now, only the great fireplace of the hall remains intact where once the great Yule log blazed during the twelve days of Christmas festivities and open-handed hospitality.

The Cunliffes lived at Wycoller Hall for centuries, a pack of sporting country squires much given to spectacular horsemanship, reckless coach-driving and devotion to the cock-pit. A certain Mistress Cunliffe once swooned when a hunted fox streaked into her chamber for safety and was savaged by the hounds before her eyes.

The last squire died in 1819, propped up in bed, it was said, to watch a cockfight laid on in his room.

Legend has it that every year, in the wild and stormy weather, a spectral horseman gallops up the dene to Wycoller Hall. His dress is of the Stuart period, his horse's trappings are careless. The rider dismounts at the door and rushes up the staircase (now decayed) to an upstairs room (now vanished). A woman's anguished screams rend the night air, then die away to a sobbing. The horseman re-appears at the door, mounts his wild-looking steed and gallops off like the wind. The tradition is that a Cunliffe murdered his lady in that room. It was she who had predicted the extinction of the family. The prophecy came true, as we now know, and the murderer seems doomed to visit, every year, the scene of his crime.

7

The Heart of Lancashire
— Mill-towns and Moorlands

Hoghton Tower and Sir Loin.

THE FORMIDABLE pile of Hoghton Tower, set on a great tree-girt hill, was the scene of royal hi-jinks in 1617 when James I and an illustrious retinue stayed here during an expensive royal progress through Lancashire. According to tradition, a red velvet carpet, half a mile long, covered the steep driveway up to the tower and the entourage was received with pipings and rush-bearings in the outer courtyard. A vast amount of rebuilding, re-furnishing and laying down of gargantuan quantities of food and wine had been organised by "Honest Dick" (Sir Richard) and the de Hoghton family were financially embarrassed thereby for generations. (A neighbour named Shuttleworth burned his house to the ground, considering that cheaper than entertaining the Sovereign).

At Hoghton Tower, in a spirit of merriment, and from a score of meat dishes on the over-loaded menu, the monarch knighted a tasty loin of beef and ever since it has been referred to as Sirloin. As the Royal cavalcade departed, "Honest Dick" took his friends down to the cellars and they were soon "as merry as Robin Hood and all his fellows"—a philosophical prelude to several years incarceration in the Fleet Prison for debt.

Another local legend connected with the visit concerned a lump of stone at the roadside, bearing a message which read: "Torne me o'er and I'le tell thee plain." It caught the king's eye and with much heaving and shoving the stone was turned. It now read: "Hot Porritch softens hard butter-cakes so torne me o're again."

Standish—Cat I'T' Window.

THERE ARE several explanations of this curious name but the most likely is connected with Catholic activities in penal times. Priests moved secretly, in imminent danger of a most barbarous end, visiting occasionally a house near Pepper Lane to celebrate the Mass. The figure of a cat placed on the window sill indicated to the faithful that a priest was on the premises.

Above: The now demolished Ince Hall. Opposite: Mab's Cross, Wigan.

Mab's Cross, Wigan.

THE BASE and stump of an old cross standing in front of a school in Standishgate, Wigan, perpetuates the memory of Lady Mabel Bradshaigh of Haigh Hall, whose mutilated effigy lies beside that of her husband, Sir William, in the Parish Church of All Saints. Sir William was absent from home and country for seven years early in the 14th century. It has been suggested that he went off to the Crusades, but it is more likely that he fled the realm after involvement in troubles much nearer home.

In time, voluntarily or otherwise, Lady Mabel married a Welsh knight, but the union brought little comfort. Years later, the unhappy lady, distributing her customary charities to the poor, noticed a palmer mingling with the crowd, whose features evoked memories of her first husband. It was indeed Sir William, returned from his adventures and hovering discreetly, to avoid embarrassment.

He revealed his identity to the tenants and, learning about the usurper's villainy, pursued the Welsh knight, overtook and slew him at Newton-le-Willows, for which crime he was outlawed for a period. The Bradshaighs were happily reunited, but Lady Mabel fared ill at the hands of her confessor who obliged her to walk "onest every week barefoot and bare legged to a crosse ner Wigan from the Haghe, which is call'd Mabb to this day."

Ince Hall and the Wicked Lawyer.

THE FINE moated, half-timbered hall, once beautifully set near Wigan on the highroad to Bolton, is no longer in existence. It was

the setting for a macabre legend about an unscrupulous lawyer and his evil scheme to defraud the rightful heirs. The owner of the hall lay dying and, wishing to execute his last will, sent for the lawyer. He arrived, however, after his client had expired. The lawyer despatched his clerk to fetch the miracle-working hand from the Gerards of Bryn whose hall was only a mile distant. The corpse was rubbed with the hand until it sufficiently revived to sign a document bequeathing the property to the lawyer.

After the funeral, the dead man's daughter discovered an unsigned will leaving everything to herself and her brother who speedily tackled the lawyer, fought him and left him, as he thought, wounded unto death. In a blind panic, the brother fled the realm, never to return, and shortly afterwards his sister mysteriously disappeared. No one knew where, or how, she had gone until a gardener turned up her skull in the garden, and all was revealed. By this time, Ince Hall was continually haunted by the ghost of the murdered girl, tormenting the lawyer wherever he went. He is said to have dragged out his days in Wigan, the victim of remorse and hallucinations.

Ashton in Makerfield and the Holy Hand.

MIRACULOUS cures have been attributed to the severed hand of Saint Edmund Arrowsmith who was put to death for his faith on Lancaster Moor in 1628. The relic is preserved in a white silken bag within a casket at St. Oswald's Roman Catholic Church. The Jesuit priest was born at Haydock in 1585, educated at Douai and ordained in 1612. He returned to Lancashire, based himself at Brindle, near Chorley, but travelled fearlessly through the county to say Mass in secret and to bind his scattered flock into the faith. He is reputed to have said his last Mass at a house in Gregson Lane, Brindle, and interesting traces of his ministry there were visible for long enough.

He was betrayed, at last, by a young woman of his own persuasion, tried and found guilty of treason. He faced death with fortitude and relics were secured and treasured, including the hand which was kept by his mother's family, the Gerards of Bryn, for many years before it was given to the priest at St. Oswald's. The saintly hand was supposed to cure all manner of sickness, including the removal of tumours, and became an object of pilgrimage to Catholics from far and wide. The hand was traditionally linked with the legend of Ince Hall.

THE HOLY HAND.

The house in Gregson Lane, Brindle, where Father Arrowsmith last said Mass

Hindley's Burning Wells.

THE BURNING wells of Hindley, which went out of existence during last century, were a matter of great curiosity to travellers. There was one in Derby Lane at the edge of a deep ditch and another at Dog Pool, later called Grange Brook, beside an old farmhouse. During a tour of Lancashire in 1676, Francis North (Baron Guildford) witnessed the phenomenon. A workman had previously dug up a turf and replaced it. Upon the arrival of the illustrious visitor, he took off the turf, applied a brown paper match and, with a little puffing, induced the hole to fill "with a blue spirituous flame like brandy."

While it was still burning, water was put into the hole when "the flame continued upon the water as if it had been spirits." Some people even claimed to have boiled eggs there. The curiosity was witnessed in 1835 when the flame appeared in a conical shape with a base as wide as a man's hat and rising to about 18 ins. high.

The Bradshaw Centenarian.

JAMES HORROCKS of Bradshaw, near Bolton, became a legend in his own lifetime. His father and mother, William and Elizabeth

Turton Tower, in which are displayed two legendary skulls.

Horrocks, married in 1743, being then aged 86 and 28 respectively. James was born in the following year so that, on his 100th birthday (25th March 1844) he was able to boast that his father (born in 1657) had been alive 186 years previously.

Curious people travelled great distances to see the centenarian whose father had lived in the days of Oliver Cromwell. James Horrocks died in September 1844 and was buried in Bradshaw Churchyard. A portrait of his parents can be seen at Turton Tower.

The Timberbottom Skulls.

ALSO TO be seen at ancient Turton Tower, once the home of Humphrey Cheetham, are two damaged skulls, of a male and a female, which were pulled out of Bradshaw Brook about 1750 and placed upon a mantelpiece at Timberbottom Farm, Turton. Peculiar manifestations, rattlings, knockings and ghostly forms, plagued the family whenever the skulls were moved. They were even flung back into the river, but to no avail.

In 1840 the farmer could stand it no longer and the skulls were decently buried in Bradshaw Churchyard, but the disturbance continued. In desperation, the skulls were dug up and returned to their old situation at Timberbottom, and peace was restored to the household. Afterwards the skulls spent many years on the family Bible in the study at Bradshaw Hall. Now they are on view at Turton Tower.

Noon Hill and the Ghostly Horseman.

THIS GRIM summit of Noon Hill, near Bolton is often shrouded in mist. It had anciently a reputation of being haunted. A trackless stony place, uncomfortable for hikers and beset by unsuspected bogs, it was by tradition the haunt of the ghostly horseman who spirited travellers away, both body and soul, and whose mount could tread the bog "without wetting a hair of his foot."

Even the natives would feel uneasy in crossing this sinister hill and would shiver as though being watched by unseen eyes. Excavations into the tumulus at Noon Hill in 1958 by the Bolton Archaeological Society brought to light evidence of Middle Bronze Age activity in the form of human remains and an urn, now displayed in Bolton Museum.

Twa Lads Hill.

IN THE WILD rough territory of Winter Hill, a few miles from Horwich, two cairns were raised on a nobbly summit in memory of two young boy shepherds who were overtaken by a snow-storm and there perished. There is evidence that the stones were plundered from existing, and possibly prehistoric, cairns in the vicinity. The Two Lads' Monument, which once resembled "huge cylinders," has since been raided and much reduced.

Scotsman's Stump.

ON A TRACK across the lonely Rivington moors a Scottish wayfarer was said to have been brutally murdered on the 9th November, 1838. Near the foot of the ITA mast on Winter Hill the event is recalled in the monument called "Scotsman's Stump." George Henderson was nineteen years of age. He had spent the previous night in Wigan. Was he wilfully murdered or accidentally shot by a poacher out in the thick November fog? A man was charged and sent to the Assizes, but was found not guilty.

The Martyr's Footprint at Smithills, Bolton

ON A flagstone in a passage leading to the chapel of this 14th century manor house appears a curious and ineradicable mark purported to be the footprint of the Rev. George Marsh of Deane, Bolton. This Protestant martyr was arrested in the reign of Mary Tudor and summoned to appear before Sir Roger Barton and others in the upper Green Chamber at Smithills Hall, where he bore much taunting and browbeating with Christian humility. Afterwards, in anger at the injustice of the proceedings, he stamped his foot upon the stone and cried out that there would always be a reminder of this day's work. He was taken away and burnt to death at Chester.

Radcliffe Tower and Fair Ellen.

RADCLIFFE, or Red Rock, goes back to Saxon times and was held by Edward the Confessor. The knightly Radcliffes came early upon the scene and several were raised to the rank of High Sheriff. Until it became ruinous, Radcliffe Tower was one of the most noble manor houses in the county. The tower was a pele of great strength with provisions for repelling attacks. The manor house was rebuilt and embattled in Henry IV's time but fell into dilapidation by the 1830s and was used latterly as a cowshed and hayloft.

It was the ancient scene of black tragedy, commemorated in the poem "Fair Ellen of Radcliffe." The first wife of the knight of Radcliffe died giving birth to a daughter, dearly loved and treasured. Ellen's outstanding beauty aroused in the second wife an obsessive jealousy. When Ellen was eighteen and at the peak of comeliness, the wicked stepmother hatched a plot to destroy her. Opportunity arose when the knight went off hunting with his friends, while his wife and daughter went to church to pray. From this hallowed place, the stepmother despatched Ellen with a message for the master-cook that he should kill the white doe from the park and prepare it for dinner.

Innocently, Ellen tripped homewards, whereupon the master-cook "streight his cruell blodye hands he on the ladye layd," knife already sharpened for its bloody business, for the "milk-white doe" was none other than the daughter of the house. Vainly the puny scullion boy begged for Ellen's life, even offering his own in poor exchange, but the butchery proceeded and the "white doe pye" was laid on the table for dinner.

The knight returned and called for his fair daughter Ellen. "Forget her," snapped the stepmother. "Into some nunnery she is gone." The distressed father vowed that he would neither eat nor drink until he had seen her for himself.

> *O then bespake the scullion boye*
> *With a loud voice so hye*
> *If now you will your daughter see*
> *My Lord, cut up that pye*
> *Wherein her fleshe is mincéd small*
> *and parchéd with the fire*

All causéd by her stepmother
Who did her death desire.

The knight mourned his loss most grievously, the wicked step-mother was burnt at the stake, the master cook was plunged into boiling lead and the poor scullion lad was made heir of all the Radcliffe lands.

The Blue Anchor Inn, Hougton, where Father Arrowsmith lodged and was betrayed (See page 58)

Rochdale Goblins.

IN SAXON times, "Recedham" was held by Gamel, Thane under
Edward the Confessor, who "for the salvation of his immortal soul"
was moved to erect a chapel dedicated to St. Chad beside the River
Roch which flows through the town. Building materials were brought
to the site, foundations were laid and the work proceeded. Then,
during one night, by some magical means, the whole mass was lifted
neatly and deposited on the summit of a steep hill across the river.
Half a hundred men lugged the materials back to the original site,
only to discover, next morning, that they had again been wafted
across to the opposite hill. It was all put down to the "goblins"
though Gamel is supposed to have interpreted these curious happenings as a sign from the Almighty that the church should stand in
its present lofty and commanding situation 123 steps above the
town.

St. Chad's Church was dedicated late in the 12th century. There
has been much re-structuring since then, and stone-cleaning and
improvements during the 1960's have revealed the true beauty of
the old church. In the church yard lie the remains of "Tim Bobbin"
(John Collier, the Milnrow schoolmaster) who took "th'owd Lonky-
sheer" dialect and turned it into an art form. He died in 1786.

The Old Packer Spout.

IN GARDENS at the foot of St. Chad's Church steps, Rochdale, the
Packer spout still exists. It is a pool now, but once it was an
ancient spring which flowed into a stone basin, and was the favourite
gossiping ground for young and old. It was the custom for a young
maiden to throw two straws into the water and count the bubbles.

Each bubble meant another year to wait before her wedding. On Palm Sunday churchgoers threw their palms into the water. If they floated, all was well. If they sank, ill fortune could be expected. In 1760 three local men piped water from the Packer Spout to the lower houses nearby. Thus it became Rochdale's first reservoir.

Toad Lane Memories.

AT THE FOOT of Toad Lane (from "T'owd Lane"), Rochdale, stands the Clock Face Inn, built on the site of the cottage where Edwin Waugh, "Poet Laureate of Lancashire" and master of the dialect, was born in 1817. He was buried in Kersal Churchyard in 1890.

Up the steep Toad Lane, the quaint three-storey building on the left commemorates the birth of the Co-operative movement. In 1844 when a group of working men, on a capital of £28, launched into mutual trading at premises vacated by the Pioneer Regiment, to the derision of their neighbours. The Pioneer Stores commenced in the true spirit of the Chartists and to combat the hard times under the Corn Laws. The movement survived initial set-backs ,prospered and spread to many countries of the world, and the building has become a historical showpiece.

Rochdale Rush Bearing.

THE AGE-OLD custom of taking fresh rushes to be strewn on the church floor for winter comfort continued in Rochdale well into last century. Up to a dozen carts, bearing rushes piled up to 24ft. from the ground, entwined with garlands and crowned with evergreens, proceeded from surrounding villages to the accompaniment of fiddle playing and dancing. A team of virile young men wearing floral wreaths, gay ribbons and white shirts drew the cart and steadied it at the rear. As a reward, they were granted the first choice of partners from amongst the prettiest girls of the district. By the 1830s only two or three carts took part in the ceremony which died, in Rochdale, with the century.

Rake Inn and the Laughing Cavalier.

ON THE right hand side of the road from Rochdale to the top of Blackstone Edge, the Rake Inn has a jolly "presence" in the form of a handsome cavalier who haunts the landing and makes the ancient rafters resound with uproarious laughter. This merry ghost with a twinkle in his eye may have some connection with "Oliver's Cottage," at the foot of the same highway, where Old Noll is reputed to have spent the night.

The inn sign bears the figure of a laughing cavalier, but this is not the origin of the "Rake," which really refers to the rough road rising to the moorlands.

Milnrow and the Clegg Hall Boggart.

BUILT ABOUT 1600 by Theophilus Ashton, Clegg Hall stands derelict by the Rochdale Canal. From 1818 to 1869 it was a public house called the "Black Sloven"—the name of a favourite hunting mare of legendary speed which belonged to a former owner, Mr. Charles Turner. He died in January, 1733, and the mare walked in the cortege carrying his hunting regalia.

Clegg Hall had a peculiar reputation and was believed to be haunted. Traditionally, a wicked uncle, guardian of the two orphaned heirs, threw the children into the moat and claimed the estate for himself. The Boggart Chamber became a place to be avoided. During the Commonwealth era, there were hints of counterfeiting activities in the vaults and cellars of Clegg Hall.

Worsley—The Wardley Hall Skull.

IN TUDOR times, Thurstan Tyldesley erected the fine half-timbered and moated manor house of Wardley Hall, Worsley, which was later purchased by a family called Downes. The last male of that line was one Roger Downes, a notable young hell-raiser and one of the "most licentious of the courtiers of Charles II." There is a legend that he lost his head, after an evening's dissipation, as he staggered over London Bridge vowing to slay the first person he encountered.

The victim was a poor tailor wending his innocent way home. A watchman who had witnessed the crime raised his bill and struck off Roger's head, heaving the body over the parapet into the Thames. The head was packaged and returned to Roger's sister at Wardley Hall, some time around 1676. Legendary tales collected about the skull, which was preserved in an embrasure between the hall and the staircase. A maidservant thought it was the skull of an animal and tossed it into the moat, and a sudden terrifying storm assailed the property. The relic was hastily retrieved and put back in its niche. Every snbsequent disturbance of the grisly exhibit brought evil happeniugs to the household.

Unfortunately for the legend, the Downes family vault

in Wigan Church was opened in 1729, and inspection revealed that, however reckless he had been in life, Roger had kept his head in death—though it was evident that a surgeon had sawn off the top of the cranium, probably during a post mortem examination to determine the cause of death.

So, whose was the skull? It possibly belonged to Ambrose Barlow of Barlow Hall, Chorlton-cum-Hardy, (converted into a golf club house), a Roman Catholic priest and friend of the Downes family, who was tried and executed at Lancaster in 1641. His severed head was impaled on the tower of Manchester's Collegiate Church until Francis Downes recovered it and took it to Wardley Hall. Father Barlow's hair had been chestnut-coloured and strands of that shade adhered to the skull for long enough, giving credence to the claim that this was the head of the martyred priest.

Worsley and the Love-Lorn Canal Builder.

DISAPPOINTMENT in love drove Francis Egerton, third Duke of Bridgewater, from the dissipations of high society life in London and Newmarket, back to Worsley and pitchforked him into a career of canal building as Lancashire teetered on the edge of the Industrial Revolution. As a clod-hopping young landowner, he

The third duke of Bridgewater.

became deeply enamoured of Elizabeth Gunning, the widowed Duchess of Hamilton. The beauty of the two Gunning sisters, Elizabeth and Maria, had taken London by storm.

Maria, wife of Lord Coventry, had meantime become involved in a scandal. The unsophisticated Duke of Bridgewater wished his intended bride to sever relations with her sister and, when Elizabeth refused, the romance came to an abrupt and painful end. From that moment, Francis withdrew from fashionable society, foreswore the company of women, and returned to his Worsley estates to ponder at leisure on the prospects of constructing a canal, from Worsley to Manchester, an idea originally conceived by his late father, Scroop Egerton, the first Duke.

The Bridgewater Canal was designed to halve the price of coal transported from the Duke's Worsley mines to the Manchester centre of manufactures, and that end was accomplished when it opened in 1761. Others followed and it is true to say that the canal system of Great Britain owes its development to the stubborn pride, or sisterly devotion, of an 18th century beauty.

Canal Designers—Brindley and Gilbert.

THE LEGENDARY canal engineer James Brindley was born into a poor family in Derbyshire in 1716. He became a mill-wright's apprentice, exhibiting outstanding skill and ingenuity in practical mechanics, though practically illiterate. His plans were generally

Dr. John Dee.

sketched in chalk on the floor. Brindley offered his services to the Duke of Bridgewater for half-a-crown a day. When, occasionally, he was confounded by the magnitude of the problems involved, he took to his bed and remained there, sometimes for days, until a solution matured in his mind.

Originally a man of sober and temperate habits, Brindley developed a fondness for extravagant living and never left the meal table until the bottom button on his waistcoat threatened to pop. He died in 1772, exhausted by excessive labour. John Gilbert, third member of the canal building triumvirate, was the Duke's steward, confidant and adviser. He has rarely been accorded full credit for his part in the great canal schemes but, when Barton Aqueduct was under construction, James Brindley foresaw disaster, took fright and ran away. It was John Gilbert who worked out a solution and saved the project.

Manchester and Dr. John Dee.

LEGENDS surrounded John Dee during his lifetime. Of Welsh descent, born in London in 1527, and a scholar of St. John's College, Cambridge, he distinguished himself in the Low Countries in mathematics and astronomy and returned to a Fellowship of Trinity College, newly founded by Henry VIII. Sinister tales of magical arts dogged his career, and he was charged with endangering Queen Mary Tudor by enchantments, but acquitted. Later, he found favour with Elizabeth I, a corner of whose cool mind was intrigued by such superstitions as the philosopher's stone, the elixir vitae, necromancy and astrology. Dr. Dee determined the most auspicious day for her coronation and, driven by vanity, he plunged into illicit commerce with the world of spirits.

His confederate for eight years was Edward Kelley. After an enraged mob had broken into the Doctor's house and destroyed his priceless library in 1583, the strange pair fled to Bohemia and lived like lords by invoking spirits and interpreting their utterances. Eventually, Dee recognised in his partner a shallow imposter and this led to a rupture. Dee returned in 1595, and Elizabeth appointed him Warden of Manchester College, a post he held for seven years. Though generally feared as a conjuror, magician and trafficker in demons, he was frequently visited by the most illustrious of the

Lancashire gentry. Nevertheless, his malodorous reputation caused him to quit Manchester for Mortlake, where his life dragged to a close in poverty and misery in 1608. (See Walton-le-Dale and Edward Kelley).

Riding the Black Lad at Ashton-Under-Lyne.

THE CEREMONY of Riding the Black Lad was held every Easter Monday, when the good folk assembled to dishonour the memory of a once dreaded and black armoured knight who had wielded his authority with the utmost severity. Ralph of Assheton received the

honour of knighthood from Henry VI and acquired the neighbouring manor of Middleton by marriage to the heiress. This reputedly cruel and violent man returned every year to inspect the manor and impose penalties on any who had failed to clear their ground of persistent weed, the corn marigold, which tyrannical interference invoked the hatred of the people. Every year after his death, a straw effigy of the black-clad oppressor was mounted upon a horse, led through the streets escorted by a procession, and afterwards used as target practice for anyone in possession of fire-arms, a custom which persisted into last century.